Martin's Dream Day

KITTY KELLEY   PHOTOGRAPHS: STANLEY TRETICK

Martin's Dream Day

Atheneum Books for Young Readers

New York   London   Toronto   Sydney   New Delhi

To every child who reads this
book—Dream Big.
—K. K.

Martin Luther King Jr. was nervous. He had been up all night writing what would become the most famous speech of his life. Now, standing at the foot of the Lincoln Memorial, he was about to address 250,000 people.

He had never seen that many people gathered in one place before. Men, women, and children were standing row upon row for blocks around him, and for one full minute he could not say a word because their applause filled the sky. They were cheering the messenger of their most cherished dreams.

Martin Luther King Jr. believed in equality. For everyone—not just a few. He wanted all people to have the full rights of citizenship. That meant the right to vote, to go to school, and to get a job. In the 1960s, African Americans did not have these basic rights. They could not eat in certain restaurants, go to certain schools, stay in certain hotels, or shop in certain stores.

Martin wanted to change all that, and he dedicated his life to making that change happen. As a minister, he preached that equality was a God-given right. That everyone—blacks and whites—deserved to be treated with the same dignity and respect. He also believed in nonviolence, so he made his demands for equality in a peaceful way. He tried to bring attention to the plight of African American people by leading marches, sit-ins, and boycotts across the South.

But his efforts for change were not enough. He knew he needed something more to make his dream come true. He decided to go to Washington, DC, to talk to the president of the United States about equal rights. "The time has come, Mr. President," Martin wrote to John F. Kennedy, "to let those dawn-like rays of freedom ... fill the heavens with the noonday sunlight of complete human dignity."

Martin made many trips to the White House with other civil rights leaders. They tried to persuade the president to propose a law that would give black people the same rights as white people. After months of meetings and many weeks of telephone calls and telegrams, President Kennedy finally agreed. He, too, believed in Martin's dream.

President Kennedy addressed the nation on television the night before he sent his civil rights bill to Congress.

"We are confronted primarily with a moral issue," he said. "It is as old as the Scriptures and is as clear as the American Constitution. . . .

"If an American, because his skin is dark, cannot eat lunch in a restaurant open to the public, if he cannot send his children to the best public school available, if he cannot vote for the public officials who will represent him . . . then who among us would be content to have the color of his skin changed and stand in his place?"

Sadly, not everyone believed in civil rights. The president's words angered those who did not want equality. Racists reacted with ugly violence. They beat up civil rights workers; they torched churches and bombed schools; they even killed a follower of Martin Luther King Jr.

Yet Congress did nothing.

But Martin did not give up. He blew the trumpet of hope. With stirring speeches, he pumped courage into those who were afraid. He proclaimed his belief in the goodwill of America. He insisted that what he called "the bank of justice" was not bankrupt, that it was full enough to give everyone a golden opportunity.

How could Martin show the lawmakers in Congress just how many people in America shared his hope for a better life? He decided that a mass protest march on Washington, DC, was the best way to make senators and representatives pay attention.

Like a general, Martin summoned troops. First, he called upon the major groups who had been fighting long and hard for civil rights: groups like the Student Nonviolent Coordinating Committee (SNCC), the Congress of Racial Equality (CORE), and the National Association for the Advancement of Colored People (NAACP). Then he reached out to churches, synagogues, and mosques because he wanted all religions to be represented. He called upon Catholics and Jews, Protestants and Muslims to gather at the foot of the Lincoln Memorial on August 28, 1963.

Martin chose the Washington Mall's magnificent white marble statue of Abraham Lincoln as their meeting place because Lincoln, known as "The Great Emancipator," had abolished slavery: His Emancipation Proclamation of 1863 had declared freedom for 3.1 million slaves. One hundred years later, Martin yearned to free the 19 million descendants of those slaves.

IN THIS TEMPLE
AS IN THE HEARTS OF THE PEOPLE
FOR WHOM HE SAVED THE UNION
THE MEMORY·OF ABRAHAM LINCOLN
IS ENSHRINED FOREVER

27

19

People all across the country responded to his call. They made plans to come to Washington on planes, trains, trucks, trailers, cars, buses, and bicycles. One man even roller-skated from Chicago!

Movie stars and musicians from Hollywood joined writers, poets, and artists. Parents brought children; teachers brought students. Farmers, firemen, policemen, secretaries, doctors, lawyers, plumbers—all came to Washington to tell Congress to pass the law that would give everyone the same rights.

21

In solidarity, people in other countries around the world declared their intention to march on August 28, in places like Berlin, Munich, Amsterdam, London, Oslo, Madrid, The Hague, Tel Aviv, Cairo, Toronto, and Kingston, Jamaica.

The march took place on a Wednesday, but people dressed as if for Sunday church. Their purpose was serious, so their clothes were proper. Women wore hats and high heels. Men wore white shirts and ties and fanned themselves with straw snap-brims.

The month of August steams with humidity in Washington, DC, but the heat did not stop hundreds of thousands of people from coming to the march. It was the largest assembly ever gathered at the feet of Lincoln, and the gathering was joyful.

People sat twenty-deep around the Reflecting Pool, where they dangled their feet in the water.

The famous singer Marian Anderson was supposed to open the program with "The Star Spangled Banner," but she could not make her way through the crush of people. So Camilla Williams, the first black woman to have a role with the New York City Opera, sang it instead. Soon, soaring music turned the Mall into an open-air cathedral and filled the skies with song.

After an afternoon of powerful speeches and solemn singing, the most magnificent moment of the day came at the end of the program when Martin Luther King Jr. appeared onstage. Applause rolled across the Mall like claps of thunder as the thirty-four-year-old preacher walked to the microphone. Women waved lace hankies and men stomped and cheered. Everyone expected something spectacular from this man, the most exciting speaker of his time. He had traveled 275,000 miles that year and given 350 speeches, trying to make America understand the desperation of its black citizens, but this audience was his biggest ever. His message would resound for years to come.

Martin began by addressing the long struggle, the terrible nights of jail and injustice. He talked about the trials and tragedies African Americans had endured. But he did not dwell on those wrongs. Instead, he urged his people not to be bitter. Not to hate, not to seek revenge.

Inspired by his words, the crowd roared its admiration. They fell quiet only when he paused for a moment. In that moment, Mahalia Jackson, a famous gospel singer, shouted:

"Tell them about the dream, Martin. The dream."

That's when Martin Luther King Jr. put aside his prepared speech. Like a bird bursting from its cage, he took flight.

"**I have a dream** that one day this nation will rise up and live out the true meaning of its creed: 'We hold these truths to be self-evident, that all men are created equal.'"

For the next fifteen minutes, Martin dazzled the crowd with his dream of brotherhood and equality. He encouraged everyone "to hew out of the mountain of despair a stone of hope." Hope pushed Martin forward—the hope for a better life. He shared his vision for a nation that would no longer be divided, but would embrace all its citizens without regard for the color of their skin.

The crowd was spellbound as Martin's voice rose to the sky, full of that hope. He told America that if it was to become a great nation, it must make the dream of freedom come true for every single person in it. He ended with the words of the old spiritual:

"Free at last! Free at last! Thank God Almighty, we are free at last."

The next year, President Lyndon B. Johnson signed into law the Civil Rights Act of 1964. A year later, he signed the Voting Rights Act of 1965.

Finally—Martin's dream had begun to come true.

STANLEY TRETICK

AUTHOR'S NOTE

I wrote this book to share the photographs of my friend Stanley Tretick (1921–1999), so children can see not simply illustrations, but real-life images from the March on Washington, August 28, 1963: that important day when more than 250,000 people gathered in the nation's capital and heard Martin Luther King Jr. give his "I Have a Dream" speech.

That day and that speech have gone down in history as the crowning glory of the civil rights movement—a movement that still needs all of us to press forward for full equality for everyone. Stanley Tretick's photos capture the soaring hopes of the crowd—the largest ever assembled on the National Mall. His images show flags flying and strangers holding hands as they petition Congress to pass a civil rights law. Through the lens of his camera, we see the spirit of hope and brotherhood that bonded people in common purpose on that day. The massive demonstration sent a message around the world that the time had come to make Martin Luther King Jr.'s dream come true for America.

Stanley Tretick was one of President Kennedy's favorite photographers; on assignment for *Look* magazine, he captured the iconic image of young John F. Kennedy Jr. playing under his father's desk in the Oval Office. Stanley saw in Martin Luther King Jr. all that he admired in John F. Kennedy: both men were inspiring leaders—visionaries, really—who understood the power of big dreams to change the world. They lost their lives in service to those dreams, but their legacies continue to inspire us.

I will be donating my proceeds from this book to Reading Is Fundamental, the largest nonprofit children's literacy organization in the United States. With this book, I hope that children will better understand the March on Washington and realize the treasure of Martin Luther King Jr.'s dream.

—Kitty Kelley

TO LEARN MORE, PLEASE VISIT:

The King Center: thekingcenter.org

Smithsonian Oral History of the March on Washington:

smithsonianmag.com/history/oral-history-march-washington-180953863

The White House Historical Association: whitehousehistory.org

PHOTO GUIDE: KNOWN AND NOTEWORTHY FIGURES

p. 10: Martin Luther King Jr. with the Reverend Eugene Carson Blake, a member of the "Big Ten"—a coalition of prominent civil rights leaders—who represented the National Council of Churches

p. 12: Martin Luther King Jr. with civil rights activist Roy Wilkins

p. 13, top: Left to right: Secretary of Labor Willard Wirtz, Floyd McKissick (Congress of Racial Equality), Mathew Ahmann (National Catholic Conference for Interracial Justice), Whitney Young (National Urban League), Martin Luther King Jr., John Lewis (Student Nonviolent Coordinating Committee), Rabbi Joachim Prinz (American Jewish Congress), Rev. Eugene Carson Blake (National Council of Churches), A. Philip Randolph (Brotherhood of Sleeping Car Porters), President John F. Kennedy, Vice President Lyndon B. Johnson, Walter Reuther (United Auto Workers), Roy Wilkins (National Association for the Advancement of Colored People)

p. 13, middle: Attorney General Robert F. Kennedy with President Kennedy

p. 13, bottom: Left to right: Rabbi Joachim Prinz; A. Philip Randolph; President Kennedy; Vice President Johnson; Walter Reuther

p. 14, and 15, at center: President Kennedy

p. 16: Left to right: Floyd McKissick, Martin Luther King Jr., Rev. Eugene Carson Blake, unknown, Rabbi Joachim Prinz, Joseph Rauh (civil rights lawyer), Whitney Young, Roy Wilkins, Walter Reuther, A. Phillip Randolph, unknown, Walter Fauntroy (local Southern Christian Leadership Conference organizer), unknown

p. 17: A police officer leads the Big Ten and other civil rights leaders through the United States Capitol

p. 19: The Big Ten at the feet of the Lincoln Memorial. Back row, from left to right: Mathew Ahmann, Rabbi Joachim Prinz, John Lewis, Eugene Carson Blake, Floyd McKissick, Walter Reuther. Front row, left to right: Whitney Young, Cleveland Robinson (not an official Big Ten member), A. Philip Randolph, Martin Luther King Jr., Roy Wilkins

atheneum ATHENEUM BOOKS FOR YOUNG READERS • An imprint of Simon & Schuster Children's Publishing Division • 1230 Avenue of the Americas, New York, New York 10020 • Text and compilation copyright © 2017 by Kitty Kelley, LLC • Photographs copyright © 2013, 2017 by the Estate of Stanley Tretick, LLC • All rights reserved, including the right of reproduction in whole or in part in any form. • ATHENEUM BOOKS FOR YOUNG READERS is a registered trademark of Simon & Schuster, Inc. • Atheneum logo is a trademark of Simon & Schuster, Inc. • For information about special discounts for bulk purchases, please contact Simon & Schuster Special Sales at 1-866-506-1949 or business@simonandschuster.com. • The Simon & Schuster Speakers Bureau can bring authors to your live event. For more information or to book an event, contact the Simon & Schuster Speakers Bureau at 1-866-248-3049 or visit our website at www.simonspeakers.com. • Book design by Sonia Chaghatzbanian • The text for this book is set in Gill Sans. • Manufactured in China • 1016 SCP • First Edition • 2 4 6 8 10 9 7 5 3 1 • Library of Congress Cataloging-in-Publication Data • Names: Kelley, Kitty, author. | Tretick, Stanley, photographer. • Title: Martin's dream day / by Kitty Kelley ; photographs by Stanley Tretick. • Description: First edition . | New York : Atheneum Books for Young Readers, [2017] • Identifiers: LCCN 2015043365 (print) | LCCN 2015044588 (eBook) | • ISBN 978-1-4814-6766-7 (hardcover) • ISBN 978-1-4814-6767-4 (eBook) • Subjects: LCSH: King, Martin Luther, Jr., 1929–1968. I have a dream—Juvenile literature. | Speeches, addresses, etc., American—Washington (D.C.)—Juvenile literature. | March on Washington for Jobs and Freedom (1963: Washington, D.C.)—Juvenile literature. | African Americans—Civil rights—History—20th century—Juvenile literature. | Civil rights movements—United States—History—20th century—Juvenile literature. Classification: LCC E185.97.K5 K45 2017 (print) | LCC E185.97.K5 (eBook) | DDC 323.092—dc23 • LC record available at lccn.loc.gov/2015043365

Many of the photographs in this book were previously published in *Let Freedom Ring: Stanley Tretick's Iconic Images of the March on Washington* by Kitty Kelley.